MY LITTLE BLACK BOOK

First published in 2021
by I-Cubed Group Ltd
4 Goodwin's Court
London WC2N 4LL

Copyright ©I-Cubed Group Ltd

Written by Jane Oremosu & Dr Maggie Semple, OBE
Published by I-Cubed Group Ltd
Designed by Dulcie Pryslopski
Photography by Evie Perfect

FOREWORD

The phrase 'little black book' has different connotations for people. A 'little black book' has contact information that is guarded, a secret journal of the owner's life, filled with amazing connections.

MY LITTLE BLACK BOOK

My Little Black Book is all about taking charge, expanding vocabulary, using the right word in the right place, at the best time.

Our journey has led us to explore a range of definitions and this book contains a selection of these, together with our own interpretations that allows us to reflect on the differences that exist in contemporary society.

We believe that language is key to understanding and talking about societal issues, particularly in relation to being a person of colour. You need My Little Black Book to communicate well with your work colleagues, friends, and family. This is a book for businesses, organisations, and you!

This book is for everyone, people who are entering the workplace and finding their identity, and it's also for people who manage teams, bombarded with ever-evolving definitions, neat phrases that limit their meaning. This is a contemporary dictionary, a global lexicon, a word book that takes the best definition, includes words that reflect today's world, it both corrects and provides solutions.

Blackness has ancient cultural roots, and each time we evoke those roots and apply them to contemporary situations, we strengthen ourselves and each other by elevating discussion. There are long overdue conversations to be had about the ways Black culture has been omitted from general debate, text and popular engagement. The legacy of Blackness within the literary canon is overlooked or interpreted in reductionist ways and subjected to manipulated ideas of what 'counts' as intellectual value.

Let's change the narrative, one word and phrase at a time. Language evolves, it is dynamic, it moves with time. A trendy acronym becomes an outdated expression. Let's get specific: BAME. You will see it in every recent report, you will trip over it as the A4 pages spew from the printer, but whilst it may be convenient it is no longer appropriate and is widely disliked for obvious reasons. It is an umbrella term and used to avoid uncomfortable conversations and reporting. It's a clumsy construct that masks the truth and is unreliable.

So, what can you use? Good question, but that's the best bit! You are listening and asking questions. You might be nervous about getting things wrong, but don't be. Let's try to find better words, words that have substance, words that matter to everyone who uses them. That is exactly what My Little Black Book is about.

Here's a good one to start with:

INCLUSIVE LANGUAGE

The use of words that deliberately include, avoid assumptions and bias around race, ethnicity, and cultural heritage. But of course, we all have views and lived experience to inform our choice of vocabulary.

And here's another:

VALUES

Through using succinct language, and through learning the words to use, we can arrive at shared values, shared goals, and understanding, rather than points of view.

And our words of encouragement:

Never be scared of what you do not know! Knowledge, acquired through reading and questioning, expands our thinking in all situations. The contemporary field of Black Studies corrects constructions of Blackness and acts as an alternative model for all academic studies generally. This addresses inter-disciplinary interests in cultural studies, sociology, the arts, literary criticism and media and film studies. In everything with everyone and everywhere you can be part of that discussion; in your workplace, in meetings with colleagues and in conversations with friends.

Jane & Maggie

CHALLENGE, CORRECT, CHANGE!

CONTENTS

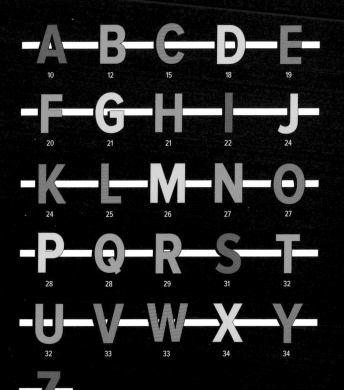

AFFINITY BIAS
The tendency for people to relate to others who share similar interests, experiences, and backgrounds.

AFRO
A hyphenated term to describe something that is said to originate from Africa.

AFRO HAIRSTYLE
Hair is curled out, forming a rounded shape.

AFRO DESCENDANT
A shortened term that refers to a person of African descent.

AFROFUTURISM
A cultural aesthetic, philosophy of science and philosophy of history that explores the developing intersection of African diaspora culture with technology.

AFRO VISIBLE
Embracing positive, beautiful images of Afro hair style.

ALLY
An individual who actively speaks out and stands up for a person or group that is discriminated against or treated unfairly; they challenge themselves, their own behaviours, and the behaviours of people around them.

ALLYSHIP
An inclusive process by members of an ingroup (own social group) emphasising social justice and inclusion of marginalised outgroups.

ANTI-SLAVERY
Opposed to the practice or system of slavery.

ATTRIBUTION BIAS
Judging a person's behaviour based on prior observations and interactions that form incorrect perceptions of them.

BAME
Black, Asian & Minority Ethnic. A term initially used for data gathering and quickly turned into a controversial acronym to describe people who are not white.

BBVP
Black British Voices Project, initiated by Maggie Semple because of her belief that the contemporary views of Black British people have yet to be understood. The project investigates the evolution of Black British identities with the aim of providing an updated portrait of Black Britishness for the 21st Century. The national survey was launched in May 2021 by I-Cubed Group Ltd, University of Cambridge and The Voice newspaper. The lead researcher is Dr Kenny Monrose, Fellow of Wolfson College, University of Cambridge.

BFLO
Black, Female Led Organisation, a term created by Jane Oremosu to recognise and acknowledge the endeavours of black women in business.

BME
Black & Minority Ethnic. A controversial acronym to describe people who are not white.

BIAS
Action, treatment, inclination, or prejudice for or against one person or group, especially in a way considered to be unfair.

BLACKISM
An ideology, mindset and positive movement promoting black people.

BLACK BRITISH
A term that people choose to describe themselves.

BLACK CONSCIOUSNESS
A mindset and way of life of black people who know their potential and value.

BLACK ENERGY
A positive aura that is strong, powerful and a force for good.

BLACK HISTORY MONTH
An annual observance originating in the United States in 1969, where it is also known as African American History Month. It has received official recognition from governments across the world. (February in the US, October in UK).

BLACK IDENTITY
A person who understands what it means to be black and the history of their heritage.

BLACK LIVES MATTER (BLM)
The collective description of the condemnation of the unjust killings of black people by police and the demand that society values the lives and humanity of black people as much as it values the lives and humanity of white people.

BLACK MIXED RACE
An assumptive categorisation based on the colour of a person's skin that one of their parents is black.

BLACK POUND
The economic power that all black people collectively have available to spend.

CODE SWITCHING
Adjusting one's style of speech, appearance, behaviour, and expression in ways that will optimise the comfort of others in exchange for fair treatment.

COLONIALISM
A practice of control by one people or power over a group of other people, by establishing colonies and with the aim of economic dominance. In the process of colonisation, colonisers impose their religion, language, economics, and other cultural practices.

COLOURISM
The practice of favouring lighter skin over darker skin.

COLOUR BLIND
A denial of thought when seeing a person's skin colour, especially black.

COLOUR BRAVE
Unafraid to have candid conversations about race that help better understand other's perspectives and experiences.

COLOUR OBSERVANT
An acceptance of thought when seeing a person's skin colour, especially black.

COMMUNITIES
Social units that group people together. While black people appear to share common characteristics they have many differences and should not be referred to singularly as the black community.

CONFIRMATION BIAS
The tendency to interpret new evidence as confirmation of one's existing beliefs or theories.

CRITICAL RACE THEORY
An academic concept that is more than 40 years old. The core idea is that race is a social construct, and that it is not merely the product of individual bias or prejudice but also something embedded in legal systems and policies.

CULTURAL APPRECIATION
When someone seeks to understand and learn about another culture to broaden their perspective and connect with others cross-culturally.

CULTURAL APPROPRIATION
The adoption of an element or elements of one culture or identity by members of another culture or identity often for economic reward or for social gravitas or kudos.

CULTURAL IDENTITY
A person's self-concept and self-perception relating to a social group that has its own distinct culture.

CULTURAL INTELLIGENCE
The state of being when someone is attuned to the values, beliefs, attitudes and behaviours of people from different cultures and responds positively to them.

CULTURAL VIBRATION
A powerful sensation felt as a result of a collective achievement or an injustice.

DEI
Diversity, equity and inclusion.

DIASPORA
Those who identify with a homeland but live outside of it.

DISCRIMINATION
Treating a person or particular group of people differently, especially in a negative way from other people.

DIVERSITY
The range of human differences.

DUAL HERITAGE
A person who has one parent who is of black heritage.

EDI
Equality, diversity, and inclusion.

E2DI
Equality, equity, diversity, and inclusion.

EQUALITY
The state of being equal, especially in status, rights, or opportunities where each individual or group of people is given the same resources or opportunities.

EQUAL PRIVILEGES
Where skin colour does not play a part in the treatment received.

EQUITY
The quality of being fair and impartial. It recognises that each person has different circumstances and allocates the exact resources and opportunities needed to reach an equal outcome.

ETHNICITY
A grouping of people who identify with each other based on shared attributes that distinguish them from other groups.

ETHNOCENTRISM
Seeing one's own culture as the correct frame of reference and way of living.

FUNDAMENTAL ATTRIBUTION ERROR
A cognitive bias. The tendency to attribute actions by another to their character or personality while not looking for the situational explanation.

GROUPTHINK

When aiming for a consensus, people set aside their own thoughts to fit in.

HALO CODE

First Afro hair code, a campaign pledge that guarantees black people in the U.K the freedom and security to wear their hair without restriction, judgement, or discrimination.

I

I-CUBED GROUP
A group of professional women who are changing the race narrative, encouraging a way of being, mindset & behaviour.

IMPLICIT BIAS
Bias that results from the tendency to process information based on unconscious associations and feelings, even when these are contrary to one's own conscious or declared beliefs.

INCLUSION
The action or state of including or of being included within a group or structure without having the need to confirm.

INDIRECT DISCRIMINATION
A practice, policy or rule that applies to everyone in the same way, but has a detrimental effect on some people more than others.

INEQUALITY
An unfair situation in society where some people have more opportunities than other people.

INTERSECTIONALITY
An analytical framework for understanding the interconnected nature of social categorisations, such as race, class, and gender as they apply to a given individual or group. It is regarded as creating overlapping and interdependent systems of discrimination or disadvantage.

INSTINCTIVELY EXCLUSIVE
Where empathy does not combine with intelligence; to act in a consciously exclusive manner from which others feel excluded.

INSTINCTIVELY INCLUSIVE
Where empathy and self-awareness combine with intelligence; to act consciously in a rational, inclusive way where others feel included.

JAZZIENESS
Someone who improvises their use of language, demonstrating the ability to adapt to different cultures.

KNEE (TAKING THE)
The action of kneeling on one knee as a symbolic gesture against racism.

LANGUAGE
The system of words, behaviour, and signs that people use to express thoughts and feelings.

LIVED EXPERIENCE
Personal knowledge about the world gained through direct, first-hand engagement in everyday events rather than through representations constructed by other people.

LUPINESQUE
To use one's blackness for good.

MICROAGGRESSIONS

Everyday slights, put-downs, and insults in the form of statements, actions or incidents that are indirect, subtle, or unintentional against members of a marginalised group such as a racial or ethnic minority.

MISOGYNOIR

A type of discrimination towards black women where both race and gender play roles in bias. The term was coined by Moya Bailey in 2008.

MULTICULTURALISM

The presence of, or support for the presence of, several distinct cultural or ethnic groups within a society.

NAME BIAS
Making negative judgements of people based on their names.

OMISSION
A failure to act. To lack the courage to be inclusive.

PERSON OF COLOUR (POC)
Someone who is not white.

POSITIVE ACTION
Taking specific steps to improve equality and equity.

POSITIVE DISCRIMINATION
When preferential treatment is given to people with a protected characteristic.

PRO BLACK
An ally of black communities.

QUOTA
A number/percentage stated to correct an imbalance of under-represented groups.

RACIAL LITERACY
Having the knowledge, skills, awareness, and disposition to talk about race and racism.

RACISM
ANTI
The policy or practice of actively opposing racism and promoting racial tolerance.

COMMODITISED
Using colour of skin overtly as an advantage to market and sell.

COVERT
The subtle but intentional and harmful attitudes or behaviours towards another person because of the colour of their skin disguised by evasive or passive methods.

INSTITUTIONAL
The collective failure of an organisation to provide an appropriate service to people because of their colour, culture, or ethnic origin.

OVERT
The intentional and/or obvious harmful attitudes or behaviours towards another person because of the colour of their skin.

RACISM
STRUCTURAL
Laws, rules, or official policies in a society that result in and support a continued unfair advantage to some people and unfair or harmful treatment of others based on the colour of their skin.

SYSTEMIC
Policies and practices that exist throughout a whole society or organisation, and that result in and support a continued unfair advantage to some people and unfair or harmful treatment of others based on the colour of their skin.

STEREOTYPE BIAS

Is maintained by biases in the attributions we make about a person's behaviour. When a person behaves in accordance with a stereotype, we attribute that behaviour to the stereotypical characteristic they share with other members of their group. This reinforces the stereotype.

SHADISM

(see colourism)

TOKENISM
The practice of making a symbolic effort to be inclusive to members of minority groups to give the appearance of racial equality.

TONE POLICING
Detracts from the validity of a statement by attacking the tone in which it was presented rather than the message itself.

UNCONSCIOUS BIAS
Prejudice or unsupported judgments in favour of or against one thing, person, or group as compared to another, in a way that is usually considered unfair.

UNCHECKED BIAS
A lack of self-awareness and thought to owning biases.

VIRTUE SIGNALLING
Describes the act of pretending to be virtuous rather than having genuine passion for an issue.

WELL SPOKEN
(see code switching)

WOKE
A term and mindset referring to self-awareness of issues that concern social justice and racial equality.

WHITE PRIVILEGE
Inherent advantages that a white person is unaware they have over a black person that automatically excludes/ protects them from certain negative experiences because they are white.

XENOPHOBIA

The fear of a stranger and often coded as a slick alternative term for racism.

YBF

An individual who is proud to identify themselves as young, black and female in the 21st Century.

YBM

An individual who is proud to identify themselves as young, black and male in the 21st Century.

YES WE CAN

"The creed that sums up the spirit of a people" Obama campaign speech.

Z

ZAPPINESS
An emotion felt by black people when celebrating, that is demonstrated by being lively, energetic, and happy.

ZEST
An enthusiasm for life leading to improved mental health.

ABOUT I-CUBED

I-Cubed creates inclusive collaborations by celebrating difference through inclusion, to inform team dynamics and for the benefit of future generations.

Our rule for businesses: we expect companies to understand change with the use of inclusive language and by continuously updating their knowledge and awareness.

We design and deliver Blacktionary workshops. Contact us for more information. Email **ic3@i-cubed.co.uk** or message us on our social channels **@icubedgroup**.

THE CREATORS

AUTHOR

JANE OREMOSU
Co-Founder and Co-CEO
jane.oremosu@i-cubed.co.uk

AUTHOR

DR MAGGIE SEMPLE OBE, FCGI, CCMI
Co-Founder and Co-CEO
maggie.semple@i-cubed.co.uk

DESIGNER

DULCIE PRYSLOPSKI
Content Creator & Marketing Director
dulcie.pryslopski@i-cubed.co.uk

NOTES

NOTES

NOTES

NOTES